PASSION AND OTHER FRUITS OF LOVE

Collected Poems

Steven H Kaplan

Printed in the United States of America.

For more information, or to book an event, contact :
AA@writechoices.com

Book design by Steven H Kaplan

ISBN: 9798335594172

First Edition: August 2024

CONTENTS

PASSION

FIRST LUNCH

I gave my affection from the start.
We shared our food in-between smiling words.
I gobbled up your charm and drank your sweet
aroma after the clinks of glasses echoed
our desire found in enduring stares;
love wrapped around the banister of deep
red roses leading up and up to when
the two of us could be alone to talk,
to gently touch and softly kiss, and kiss
each other hard until we merged as one.

Though you are far away, my love for you
cuts deep, and I still treasure the memories
of happy days and nights. Oh, how you made
me feel so special, glad to be alive.

ISLAND GIRL

The fine White Sand Beach of Koh Samed
sparkles like your brilliant smile.
We frolic down the coconut palm lined coast
and cool our feet in the refreshing surf.

I suck the fresh milk of a young coconut
to quench my thirst in the noon sun,
and you eat the delicate fruit
to satisfy your hunger.

Our dreamland invites us to swim
and wash away the dirt from past affairs.
I carry you into this bay of love
and hold your soft skin next to mine.

As you reach over and put your hand over
my heart, I desire only you and this Island.
The turquoise water urges us deeper
into another world of reefs and colorful sea life.

We come out and dry off. Me in my white skin
and blue shorts, you with your brown skin,
yellow T-shirt, black shorts, and my green hat
to shelter you from the sun's glare.

We lay down in the shade and find ourselves alone
with the wind whispering through the coconut palms,
the soft laps of the surf, and gentle kisses
to lead the afternoon sun as it bids farewell to the hot day.

The sky cools when the sun drips down
the horizon like the tear crawling down your face,
leaving a trail for the night to soak
up with silent hugs confirming I must leave.

My sunburn hurts to touch
but will heal as our time
together fades to a fond memory
of a happier day.

ANGEL WINGS

When the wings of an Angel
swoops down on his heart,
a bright grin lights his path
of wanting to be a better person.

Deep down inside, he knows
that her caring smile has touched
him with wisdom that is sweet
like the honeycomb shared on their first date.

Perhaps she is waiting for him
to return to share his life
with her. Time flies forward
while he is out earning his own wings

by doing the right thing,
overcoming his weaknesses
and counting his blessings
that he has met an Angel.

QUEST FOR KNOWLEDGE

Our eyes bond during class as we exchange
unspoken comments about the lecture.
Then I drift down a magical current,
timeless like a gurgling dream. I gently
waken from my distant slumber, a far
away reality that floats on a raft
of sparkling wit lost in my past. A giddy
shyness dwarfs my discovery of you
as I search your soul to see what you see,
to understand what you feel, to know
what you think. My heart flutters as it raises
my soul for a flirtatious peak at yours.

Within our shared space, your green eyes
smile, yet I do not understand. Intrigue leads
me down the stairs to the vending machines
where I hope to converse with you.
I settle for a glimpse, preferring to wait
until class ends when I inquire, question,
and pursue knowledge filled with your passion.

STUDYING SHAKESPEARE

My admirer sits and stares, shaking
my concentration as I read Shakespeare's
romantic sonnet "Let me not to the
marriage of true minds." Her blue eyes read my
distraction as her unswerving face glows
with rosy expectations learned from life.
The anthology, filled with articulated
experiences and lives of English poets,
gathered for posterity to interpret
meaning, relevant couplets among the
metered quatrains designed to wet my thirst
for rhymed meter and arousing metaphors.
She buries his face in paper and pen
to pull me closer to his throbbing heart.

PUCKER

Hello sweetheart, come on in,
I want to take you for a spin,
sing you a moonlit hymn,
And then kiss you on the chin.

One wild and puckering smack,
will set you right on track,
making you want to come back,
and keep you on a one-man track,

for more passion filled nights
laced with sensuous bites.
I'm sure to take you to new heights
as I hold you very tight.

CURVES

I lay in bed and remember pulling you close,
wrapping my arms around your tender body
and holding you firmly, glue like, never
let you go. I softly kiss your lips,
gradually pressing harder and faster.
You kiss me back with the passion
of wanting to merge with me.

I gently kiss my way from your soft cheek
down to your neck. You lift off your blouse
and I unbutton your bra, pulling it away
from your chest, revealing the most beautiful
breast in the world. I begin kissing you,
open my mouth wide, and take
your luscious flesh into me. Your soft
moans guide my sucking lips as the sweet skin
stimulate my taste buds. The edge
of my tongue licks your nipple as you stroke
my hair. I lick my way across your chest
to your other breast as you call out my name.

I walk my lips slowly down your stomach,
opening and closing my mouth as I feel
every inch of your luscious skin.
I memorize every curve of your delicate body.

I remember gently spreading your legs
as you lay naked in front of me.
I kiss your hips and follow your curves
inside until I reach your femininity.
My tongue leads the way as it inches
towards your erogenous zones.
At first with one deliberate lick,
then another, I increase my tempo
until you call out my name
and tell me that you love me.

You beg me to enter you with my manhood.
I keep licking you, enclosing my mouth
around your pleasure until you are ready
to climax. I climb on top of you and thrust
ecstasy into your body, sliding in and out
with perfect unison with your movements.
I control my pleasure to prolong
this heavenly moment. When you wrap
your sexy legs around my torso,
as if to keep me inside you forever.

FRIED MUSSELS ON A HALF SHELL BEACH

We melt on the rocks,
fried mussels on a half shell beach,
baking our soft and eager minds
in the afternoon sun.

We stare at the electric waves
frozen in meditation
for an eternal moment.
And in successive moments,

Mother Earth's womb, the ocean
gives birth to the surf,
delivering waves filled
with energy, alive and pounding

the sandy ground coated with children
hiding behind broken shells and suntan lotion;
they seek love and change color
just as we adapt to live another day.

The sun sets and turns the air
into a dusky paradox between
love and survival; each fights
for domination. We give and take as the tidal

current challenges the surf,
pulling and pushing back and forth.
We let love and survival edge in
to replace the outer light with our heart's light.

GROUPIE

Melancholic, hyperactive
I depend upon their music
to blow winds and sail me up high,
racing passions past joy. Like a

lover, I'm devoted to their
living dream of fusing nature
with soft harmony. I crave the
rhythm as they make love to their

instruments for all to hear. I
follow them on tour, commune with
their music, adopt their lyrics,
sing their songs, and dance to the beat.

Swaying with the stage lights in this
dark arena, I pretend they
play to me, and imagine
singing with them on the pulpit.

Valentine

The daytime dreams,
the nighttime moves,
I kiss sweet life,
and taste your soul
still in the bed-
room holding firm
our heaven filled
desires on earth.

THE BEE'S MARRIAGE

My body buzzes erotic
sounds which stimulate
excitement through a flower.
And as an aroused lover,
when his partner tongues his ear,
the epidermis senses chills
of tingling pleasure travelling
down to the tips of the roots.

Aware of myself and my needs,
aware of the flower and her needs,
we innately share our lives
married together for our existence.
Like the son of a king
who is destined to marry a princess,
I must perform my mission.
While bumbling inside of the flower,
I gather sweet nectar.
Leaving now, I am filled.

WRITER'S LOVE

I hold your poetry
in my heart, and I read
your emotions captured on paper.
I use your words and return
the passion with my own
fervent lines mirroring
your feelings with understanding.

I read the fear of future pain
tugging your heart to slow
your journey with old wounds.
Flowing red with corrections.
I wait, patient and hopeful,
for your next rewrite.

EYES

When I look in your alluring eyes,
I see a beautiful woman trying to escape
into the arms of a gentle and caring man.
Soft skin surrounds your heart,
golden like the morning sun
that renews warmth to my spirit
as it grows larger and stronger each day.

Do you remember the chocolate flower
I gave you? The chocolate represents
all the sweetness you deserve. The rose
compliments your beauty and symbolizes
your freshness that I want to hold
and nurture with tender strength and love.

The petals soak up the sun
like a special friend who listens
to your hopes and dreams,
your fears and frustrations,
the sadness and joy found
deep within you,
ready to shine with the support
of a smile that reflects
from your alluring eyes

LIFE SONG

I play another song that reminds me
of the love we once shared. Like the singer,
I desire only you. I hope you save me
a place in your heart when we are apart.

I imagine you lying naked beside
me, sharing the magic of life with our
own songs, sweet with mutual satisfaction,
a sense of belonging and forming a union

that reaches greater heights than ourselves alone.
Your presence soothes my pas as I hold you
close to me, discussing how we will hold
our child as partners on this island of life.

As I edit my lyrics, I watch you work
at your computer. My big grin brightens
the room as your fingers type your report
for school, trying to make your dreams come true.

Pride fills by common goals to pursue
our dreams. You encourage me to keep writing
and trying to sell my lyrics; you believe
my beats. Without you, I will fade and die

on this island of pain, an incomplete
life song. You brought the notes that tuned my soul,
raised my spirit, and made me stand and dance
as one with you, the woman of my dreams.

SPA

A simple gaze, that we locked with love
and joy as you shampoo away my worries.
Time stops, and my thoughts love your smile
and caring eyes that embrace with mine.

You massaged rose scented conditioner
That softens my slightly gray hair
Your firm fingers release my Internal anger
That flows away as I relax under your fingers

running over aging locks with split ends,
The past washes away with a rinse,
warm and tingling with joy. I see
the key for happiness in her heart.

most of my stress washed away,
though lingers from not being able
to reach up and touch your body,
as you reach my heart and uncover lost joy.

I could not help falling in love with you,
I wish I had met you earlier,
when my hair was longer and thicker,
before we each had spouses with dyed hair

Separation

WILD FLOWER

He flew away to work on the pipeline
And told hėr that he would be ready
To water and fertilize her when he returned.
He returned, but she was not there for him.

Somewhere out the field she used to stand tall,
the brightest flower blooming just for me.
I wandered off too many times
in search of knowledge and money,
not of other flowers, but for inner strength
so that I could protect my flower
for a long lifetime of happiness.
But she still felt lonely
sitting on that mound, wilting
from lack of water and sunlight
to nourish her, a soul, flower, deep roots
and she found someone else to fertilize
the ground where she was planted,
her petals able to thrive with bright colors

He can't see her now, gone with another who picked
Her up, not knowing her past and promises.
He sits alone in the field, pondering his quest
for knowledge and strength; while successful,
He lost the beauty that he had gained
Having learned to accept what was not
his possession, but a part of him wherever he went.
All he can do is go away and let himself heal
the cuts and bruises from a distant he gained
while pruning with memories.

PLUNGING TO HELL

Thoughts consume me, wanting her, Hot desire,
a picture of me pulling her close, One arm
around her as our willing hearts lock
In sync, a magnetic yin and yang.

Our standing hug captured forever by a selfy.
We are naked in truth, hot passionate embrace
under the stars, sheltered from the noise
and hostility of a warring world within ourselves.

She stops her unhappy time, alone in herself,
with a family that is not hers. She clings
to hopes of a lifeline to prevent her plunging
Into melancholy, a place with no love or sunshine.

During empty times, jealously invades him with pain,
Consumes, burns everything the flame contacts.
A crispy flake that brakes apart with any stress
He screams to release the smoldering pain

and collapse, almost dead, from toxic fumes
Last night's text cracks the bridge
over love's ravine. She needs a break,
a chance to refresh her breath, calm her heart

from pittering and pattering elevated beats,
that raises her up. Yet words smolder and fall
from this bridge which others try to drive
between us and suppresses our joy.

Love filled his head and heart, driving his body
Every flower reminds him of her radiating
beauty and joy. He imagines building a garden
together, filled with delicate yellow petals lining edges.

Thought of losing her to a lie dries his soul,
As if the good shrivels, dehydrated of love.
He is awake, silent and stunned, worried
that he gives all and still might lose the joy

that blossomed in the warm spring before the hot
passionate desert summer drives him into delirium
as he ponders the fall of their lives. Holding hands
and loving as they make changes, aging with maturity,

wisdom, joy. A little fertilizer and water helps
nourish our love and elevates ourselves to bliss,
high above the gates of hell, fearful the heat will stop.
Does she want to marry me like I want to marry her?

A SINGLE WHITE ROSE

He came to her office with a single
white rose that he had picked,
the healthiest from the bunch,
blooming tall and bright,
open for the world to envy.

The flower spoke from his heart,
gently telling her about the journey
to her desk, the miles of road he navigated
to arrive at her side free and strong.

She places it in the middle of her desk,
where paperwork waiting for her signature
of approval surrounds it.
The rose reaches above the clutter
to shine as it meets the incoming
morning sunlight. Its petals sparkle
as the morning light warms all it touches.

The day grows on with answered telephone calls
and adding machines advancing its paper roll.
She glances at the rose when she paused
from shuffling her paperwork
to smell the fresh scent. Yes, it is nice,
for the moment.

She brushes her hand against a thorn
and quickly pulls away,
reaching for a telephone to complain
that he wasn't more careful to trim his rose,
to protect her from himself.

The rose quietly spreads its petals wide
as the afternoon inches away.
The sun leaves, allowing
illuminated reflections from
cold spreadsheets to cover the petals,
once pure with love. Its edges fringe
after the neglect she gave.
The weight weakens the dehydrating stem,
causing the flower to weep from its own weight.
All she does is stand up, put on her sweater,
and turn off the lights,
leaving the single white rose for the janitor.

PET CEMETERY

Under grays skies,
my sweaty palms
hold a shovel full of dirt
to bury all the joy I used to know.

I gave it to you for safe keeping
and you starved my faithful
companion with deceit and lies,
spending the dog food money

on beer and other men.
I wish I could resurrect
our love, but I need you
to reach out for me

and give us new life,
with a puppy that can
reincarnate our smiles with
the innocence of starting over.

Moral Yin and Yang

WHITE

The fine line separating black
from white blends to gray when I mix
remembrances of commitment with
fiery thoughts of caressing your smooth Asian skin.
I lay back, floating on a bed filled
with your warm lips tasting my tingling skin.

Submerged inside my upbringing,
a battle wages between the safety I learned
as proper social behavior and what I learned
to accept as truth: that following my heart,
chasing my desire, to make love with you,
is where the tides of my passion lead.

My heart meanders outwards,
seeking to flood my needs with nutritious kisses.
I will myself to let conflicting faces feed
on the sweet richness given in unknown competition.
I tell myself that juggling two loves
seems wrong, even though it feels natural.

A thrusting gust dampens the fertile
boundaries between right and wrong,
littering the pure beach of giving with mud.
Is it love? Is it affection? Or does
an empty heart pretend to fill a swirling void
swimming in the shallows of a sexy pond?

Tonight I swim in the sea of marriage.
Tomorrow, I lay on my mistress's shores.
I open a bottle of champagne with each,
yet I satisfy my thirst with only half the bottle.
The glare of twilight casts a dull sparkle
on the crystal flutes, where does darkness lead?

BLACK

I lose everything I did not tie down
as roaring rapids flip me over and suck
me down in my own lies. I gasp for air
and try to fill my lungs, but a line wraps
around my throat. I prefer to cut myself off
rather than drag another soul under.

I inflate my life preserver and realize
that only the truth can keep me afloat.
The gasping pain of ignoring my honest
feelings on this ebbing sea of life
has always been true in my heart, to you
ready to ride only your red wave.

The morning reveals a hazy shore.
Truth calls out for change, yet I am torn
with the pain I caused her and the happiness
I feel when I hear your voice and reread
your letters. I paddle slowly, even though
my heart races forward to your silky shore.

DARK CHOCOLATE

As twilight falls, casting a faint glimmer
off a box of chocolates wrapped with red
ribbon and a bow, you accept the box
of empty calories with a controlled glow.

Every subtle piece melts in your moist mouth
as your smile melts my heart with creamy chews,
softly stimulating the flowery buds
on my tongue with explosions of passion

fruit. Juicy kisses build a steamy
embrace where we blend fantasy flavors
with promises of raising a family.
Once we eat every piece, our sweet love turns

to sickness, an emptiness in the gut
as we no longer share the feelings we cherished.
After your gone, the lost dessert leaves a
cavity deep within my bitter heart.

LOST WINTER LOVE

She would call me in the evening
and ask if she could come over.
With her hair around her shoulder,
I greeted her when she walked in the door
She'd smile with her eyes and give me hug,
Then we'd sit on the couch, my arms around her,
her head resting in my chest.
While we talked and smile,
I lock the door and lay besides her
As the night lengthens, we talk no more.

I still believe she comes at night
To love me, to keep me alive
With her arms around me
Until I reach to stroke her arms,
And notice the season getting later
Only distant vespers ringing
Through the cold and lonely night.

WORDS FOR GOODBYE

You know that old cliché
that "I want you everyday,"
has worn down dry,
for I can no longer try
to pretend that our habit
reflects true love's perfect fit.
Although I'm on my way out,
I still have time to pout.
Baby now that I know it's time for me to go,
please don't beg me to stay
nor offer me a lay,
for I must be on my way.

CLOUDY PAST

When his past clouds her heart
with dark and sad affairs,
the rain falls from her eyes
onto an empty and soiled bed.

They once shared sagging
springs and satin nights
embraced by their speeding hearts,
consumed with eternity.

Stained memories remain of their loving labor.
Even bleach can't wash those away.
She hangs her laundry and waits
for the spring sun to dry her cloudy past.

THE PATCH

Mending deficiencies in your
array, I weaved in and out through
the ordered columns of your scarred
attire. When tears dripped down the fabric,
I covered your worn apparel
with a strong, supportive blanket
that hid your delicate skin from
sight and exposure. My solid
soft colors sheltered you from cold
hard cotton which blended
with trends and seemed to promise fresh
flowered designs. I soon discovered
myself stripped of worn jeans
as I dangled from a single
thread your apparently forgot.
Cut me off or sew me on tight.

LEAVING OUR BED

I wake up and see your droopy eyes
begging me to end your pain. I put my arms
around you and pull your shivering
body close to me on this winter morning.

The warmth I give seems fleeting, lost
during the wet night in this damp cabin
where my darkness stops me from holding
you tight and saying that I will never let you go.

A gushing sadness pushes away my
confidence as I ponder whether I am making
the best decision of packing my gear
to pursue happiness along a separate path

where my spirit can roam freely, exploring life anew.
I look back for a rope to pull you over to my path,
yet I find no footing for you stand beside me.
My shoes glide easily over this gravely road

leading to a dreamland filled with green pastures
and gentle cascades flowing with revitalizing life.
I carry hope and scars on my back
as I begin my new journey towards summer.

I imagine another mate with eyes that touch my soul
waiting for me to arrive at my destination.
I wonder whether I walk towards a waking dream
or move in circles around an illusive fantasy.

I look back and see your painful tears
pleading to take you with me. I leave you
in bed as I take a cold shower
that distracts my wandering heart.

I lose my appetite in this chilling morning. Coffee
cold and bitter coffee stains the counter.
I eat a mango and a bowl of cereal.
I stand in the doorway, remembering past Joy.

FUEL LEAK

Fragments of my shattered heart
slice the fuel line of our love,
causing precious fuel to leak
a steamy trail of evaporating
promises on this rolling highway
once paved with commitment.

Fumes of the past fill my tank
as I coast downhill, waiting
to see you along the roadside,
returning to pump more love
or sever the line completely,
leaving me to abandon my
vehicle on this deserted road.

Steven H Kaplan

SOILED COUCH

I reach for the light blurred by the shadows
of four white walls casting a dull reflection
of my selfish desires to force my wife
to satisfy my sexual appetite.

Her skin, warming in the light has hardened
with the coming of night. Instead of her
perfumed neck, I now smell the couch reeking
of stale foam and soiled upholstery.

Torn fabric covers a cushion flattened
from neglect. Every movement chafes
her willingness to stay with me. The noose
of loneliness grates deep inside myself.

INNAUGRAL FLIGHT

On this star filled night,
I'm inaugurated
into spurned elitism.
Anger comes from rejection
for teaching you to fly
with the hope of one day soaring with you;
now I look up to see you
date another man.

The stars suspected
that you would one day fly,
even when I first wooed you
with sweet words about the highs
you would feel with me
as moon beams filled our bed.

The voice message you left
says that you did not believe me
when I told you how much I wanted
to be your copilot on this journey.

My caring
drops
from my heart
to my stomach
twisting, twisting,
as it falls.
I told you that I wanted to be with you.

Clouds hide the moon above the rain,
grounding my heart, forever changed
by the times we soared higher
than I ever thought possible.

Still, I tune my engine and clean my wings
with hope that one day I will leave
this lonely hanger and find you
ready to refuel and take off
to new heights
with me as your navigator.

ROCKET SHIP

In my speeding rocket ship
Hot flashing lights
and twinkling stars
blind my focus until
my auto pilot and your
light guide my path
Into orbit around your wholeness
Missing, yet void
of a stable landing zone.

My eyes blinded by the continued
by flashing lights and twinkling stars.
With your light guiding my path
and my auto-pilot activated,
I orbited your massive wholeness
never finding a stable landing zone.
You raise your passion to break
through your atmosphere and
rendezvous in unchartered
romantic exploration.

I dim my own lights
until my eyes can focus
on the switch that turns off my auto-pilot.
As my vision returns,
I regain control
and navigate my ship
back to the point

where I overshot you.
I noticed your distant concern,
lacking the once bright shine
that you radiated from your core,
a warm heart lined with innocence.
Solar flares erupt from your surface.
Did my lack of affection create
those flares or do they lie
deeper with failed expectations?

As my orbit slows,
the ship's instruments alert
me to a weaker gravitational pull.
Our love seems to drift away
with nothing in space to grab hold.
My caring heart drops into my stomach,
a sickness that only more space can heal.

LEFTOVERS

It's Sunday morning and I open
the refrigerator looking for breakfast
to nourish my soul.
The leftovers look stale,
a stew of half-bitten chunks
already one day too old,
dried with streaks of gristle and bone.
My stomach turns away,
not because of the quality of the food,
rather, because the food was ordered
by another man, a nameless man,
who ate sweet pleasures from
the feast you cooked up.

I love the dishes you serve,
A nourishing spread
of vitamin filled ingredients.
Your aroma fills the air
with a delicate bouquet
of candied roses blooming with desire.
Your beauty surpasses
All the other meals
I have ever seen or tasted.

Though hungry for your affection,
the leftovers seem so unappetizing.
As the freshness fades
with the smooth glaze of hardening sauces.

Call it pride or call it jealousy,
I'd rather go hungry,
starved with unfulfilled emotions
demanding to be your one and only.
My appetite vanishes
when I think of taking what
someone else was too full to finish.

My heart shouldn't be served
until you crave the organic meal
I fully seasoned and baked
With the only additives being love and intent

SELF CENTERED BATTLE

I charge up Ego Mountain,
Advancing forward, head strong
with confidence that I could do no wrong
as long as I followed my heart.

The swift resistance to my advances
Drive me to retreat to my bunker
Where I dig in deep, ready
To fend off your march out the door.

I charged once more, taking hits
along the way, wild emotional swings.
I seemed to have lost myself in this thick
battle, a confrontation of wills

Where bruised emotions claw
at any movement or speech.
From desperation point,
I counter attack with changed tactics.

Deceit and manipulation spray the air
with clusters of fragmented accusations,
hot and double edged, slicing
through and tearing tender flesh.

I slip on a soft edge and fall
into a crater, the pit I created
with the unfaithful bomb
I had dropped on you.

Desperately scrambling up the muddy side,
I climb out and notice that you're
not paying attentions to me.
Amidst the serenity of the cease fire

I make a list goals to share,
love, and listen to you,
not forcing you to be mine,
nor will I fabricate stories

to shield my heart from being shredded.
Accusations of spreading false love
cut me down; insinuations of infidelity
seep out from my remaining purity

As the chilled wind flowing from
your greener pastures curdles
red hope, a dark glob on ground
lying next to me on this battlefield of love.

JACUZZI

Hidden under her soft voice that warm
my soul as we sit in this bubbling water
and relax our tired bodies, I fill the flutes
with imported sparkling wine, the real stuff
from France. Each sip of Champagne
numbs the silence covered tension.

My mind wanders back to the past,
a dream like state filled with hope
that our knotted muscles
and the stress between us is gone,
leaving only the wobbliness
that follows a soothing massage.

I give you a smile that you timidly accept,
protecting your soul from past pain.
Deep down, I know that the time we spend
healing in this Jacuzzi will ease the silence
with sweet sounds of a gentle wind
blowing through the trees and cleaning

the night air to reveal a starry sky.
At first, we talk about constellations
we recognize, then, we create our own.
Soon the bubbles blend with our blood
as we form our own intoxicating dream
and enjoy a peaceful life together.

The bubbles shut off as our skin,
wrinkled with time, aging through
wet and warm hours of frozen time.
The night air seems to have gotten cold;
we step away from each other, quick
to dry ourselves with our own towels.

VOLCANIC ROMANCE

Molten Lava condenses the
sulfur dioxide trapped beneath
a crusty love affair. Bubbling
emotions ooze through the long cracks.

My heart erupts with gas blowing
the top of the relationship when
unfaithfulness fills the narrow
fissures with broken commitments.

Dark ashes scatter across dry white skin,
clogging my affection from pouring out.
Jealous lava boils over the edges
scathing the green landscape,

killing what was left of fertile love.
Hollow pumice cools, and cools some more,
ready to erode as the next storm
approaches with distant clouds.

GARDEN OF LOVE

(Inspired by William Blake)

Take these deep red roses and smell
the delicate aroma, sweet with the warm sun,
crisp with the morning air. A lone spring brook
meanders through a meadow lush with sacred grass.

Give me your hand my dear and let me slip
into the soft green grass of your eyes
where we will stroll along the budding paths
blossoming in your heart.

My eyes plunge deep, penetrating your soul,
only to find your soiled love for another
poisoning our Garden of Love
under briers bound with chapel liars.

AT LAST, MY DUCHESS

(Inspired by Robert Browning)

Duchess, oh my Duchess on the wall,
in the candle lit room I gaze
at your beauty captured in concrete image.
Our lost love preserved for infinity
within the framed work of another's hand.
I finally have you forever.

Day dreamed memories glare off
the framed glass recalling life
once locked in my heart
now broken with lost love.
Long curly blonde hair and tight blue eyes
shadowed by your beret
and your leather jacket
dangling down to your thighs
all hide flawed love;
you gave away the family
jewels I paid for with my heart.

You seductively unbuckle
your chastity and drop your sacred vows,
leaving me filled with sharp anger
to bury with the aged leather.
Death has replaced sex
as I free you from me at last, my Duchess,
and I leave the smashed poster for the maid.

PHOTOGRAPHY CLASS

Statistics drill past my mind,

reflecting datum from thinking machines.

I glance over through the clear glass

held tight in frame; the instant focus

tunes clear picture love in high definition.

I open wide my shutter eyes and then

erect my tripod tall with posture. One click,

she's gone forever walking down the hall.

DREAMING ALONE

(inspiration Jim Croce lyrics)

Couples stroll along the evening path
lined with wild and sweet flowers, blooming wide
and bright like the smile you used to give me.
Now I substitute the smiles with swollen
eyes and memories of laughs and the love
that I thought would save me from my self forged
steel shackles of time dragging me behind.
Last night I dreamed of you again, just like
the night before. Soft and warm, you told me
that you thought it over and said that you
were coming home; then I woke up and found
myself sweaty and cold, dreaming alone.

Despair

TRASH DAY

This thin window doesn't help me to sleep
when you clang those cans of cash
like a banker updating his debit column.
Can't you keep quiet, and be careful
with what's left of those china plates?
They were my wedding present.
Wait a minute. Don't leave.
I want to tell you about those pieces.

I had swept them up after my wife
complained of the mess I made, you see,
I rarely cleaned up my messes and usually
kept cluttering up our bedroom,
and living room with leftovers,
torn clothes, and broken vows.
One day, I wasn't paying attention
and knocked over our serving platter,
I hid the pieces into the corner closet,
the one where I stored all my collections,
souvenirs from past affairs.

Don't leave, I've got some more cans,
let me finish my story,
my wife asked where the platter went,
I denied any knowledge of it.

I wasn't home when she needed to store
old photos in the closet and found

the plate. She complained of the mess
and left me alone to clean.
I kept gluing the big pieces back,
yet before I finished, she dumped
the plate full of love into the trash.

Last night I returned to this very dumpster,
glue in one hand, broken pieces in the other,
the damage I had done
resembled jagged edges in the night.
Each piece drying in place,
I brought it back to her pantry,
only to have her refuse the plate.
I returned outside and noticed her hot eyes
looking down from the balcony,
as if evaluating my intent to fully repair
the cracks with stronger glue.

She said that she will consider
putting the plate back on her shelf.
Can you see that I need to buff
and smooth the edges?

How now? Are you confused
that I gave up so easily at the first light.
I've been going in and out until
sleep overcame me.
I left the plate before her bed.
She must have thrown it out while I slept.

I ring her doorbell and beg her to
take back this prize possession,
yet she tells me firmly that it
no longer matches the set.
I expect the garbage men to come soon,
Meanwhile, I hope that some new lover
does not bring his finest china into my home.
Here you go my friend, careful,
you don't want to break the bottles
before you get them to the recycling center.

NIGHT ARROW

Holding your hand during the moonlit hike,
filled with beams of fantasy in my Heart,
ready to sacrifice for the cause of love,
Innocent and pure within me.

Hit by arrow from behind.
I look up and don't see anyone
except you and you have no bow in your hands.
So, I pause, unsure, partially alert.

We walk some more an I'm hit again.
I don't have the strength to grip the arrow
and yank it out. I tried to ease the pain and
not let the sharp barbs rip the surrounding flesh

The barb cuts flesh as I slowly pull out
the arrow with a seething pain
Controlled in stags with each breath intensifies
I take it like a man, by standing firm on the trail

Not leaving my post, being by your side
Until you properly relieve me by telling me
that you don't want me. I look around
and drop to my knees from shock
and disbelief of your treacherous soul.

BED OF MEMORIES

I close the bungalow door and walk out
to meet the burning sun standing alone
in a sky full of hidden stars. Rays beat
down my path, unhindered by the cloudless sky.
Flies buzz me, landing on my sweaty skin
and taking off before I can strike.
More flies come and go, and come back.

The oily sand watches coconut palms dance
with the offshore breeze. I sit still,
like a charred tree trunk still rooted to the ground,
naked of the green leaves of life
and sweet fruits of happiness.
Snack vendors drudge up and down the beach;
they pass over me, ignoring me
as if I was debris washed up from the storm last night,
or last year.

A blanket of sand wraps itself
around me when I lay back.
The double bed in my bungalow,
a worn mattress, thin against the wooden frame,
a single sheet, and two pillows
all wait for me to return
with memories of cuddles, a past dream,
a lonely wish for tomorrow
when I will wake up and find the short,
dark skinned South East Asian girl
there with open arms. "Come, my love.

Come to me, my sweet."
I wake from tormented sleep
with her name on my lips.
where have you gone, Thuy?
I stay in bed, afraid that if I wake she will be gone.

Where did she go?
I walk slowly;
one foot sloshes after another.
I drag my droopy eyes
and sun cooked skin,
red flesh mixed with burnt meat
surrounding a hollowed chest
of dusty bones stained with tears.

Barbecued squid and sticky rice
slide down my throat like the sun
slipping out of the sky's grasp, falling
beyond the horizon into the unknown.

I guzzle a beer into oblivion
as the sun drops from view.
A taste of light lingers,
afraid of being consumed
by the sleepy night to suffocate
alone in a bed full of memories.
The wind shouts, "Where did she go?
Where did she go?"
This thin window doesn't help me to sleep
Soundly when you clang those cans.

FLICKER

The orange flame flickers
as it burns deep indigo wax
into a fading light for her,
their love for each other is now lax.

I recite that sacred chant,
"Their love forever banished,
now they fully recant
leaving them empty and famished."

The wick holds the flame
that evaporates how they cared,
burning away the same
desires, a love they once shared.

Lost interest ignites
memories of their past,
leaving them alone at night
as they turn their backs at last.

The uncertainties that came
with the discovery of infidelity,
lies she concocted to tame
her insecurities with levity

that dissolves into smoky air.
"None of their love remains.
Now I come to fill her with care
as I give her my Leo mane."

SPIDER HOUSE

Pain, pain, lurking in the shadows,

waiting to tear out my tender heart

and drag it slowly through solitude

and toss it down into a black crevice,

a narrow hallway

lined with silky negligées,

a web of sticky lies

ready to bind my oozing flesh

until it dries

a lump of rotting mass suspended

over a burnt mirror

reflecting the shell of a man,

a charred soul hallowed out

for baby spiders to thrive.

FALLEN

This empty bed haunts me
with your broken promise to keep
my sleep free from lonely nights
beneath the stars fading with time.

On that sunny October Sunday
when the afternoon lunch
lead to a warm evening,
you came to me,
body of a goddess,
face of an angel
with a smile that melted
my unfulfilled desires
and brought light to the night.

Laying on my side,
I stare at the framed picture
on the nightstand.
We both wore shorts, a T-shirt,
and a smile while at the amusement park,
where our beating hearts quickened
with the rushing of the roller coaster.

The picture of us at Seaworld
helps me to escape
my own emotional roller coaster
riding the emptiness of this bed.

I dream of sleeping with you
every night and day as we
massage away the tensions
affecting our well-being.

Now all those dreams I saved
in my hope chest have been crushed,
flatten with the steps of another man
whom I did not even know was there.

The deceit and broken trust
dulled the stars.
Perhaps it was only the clouds
that obscured my view,
or maybe the bedroom window needs cleaning.
The mattress deflates,
flattened with the lost love.

DEMONS

I've got our wedding photos, he's got you
I never had a chance to fight for you
As I wonder which of us, you or me,
needs protection from the ideas in my head

The terrorist strikes from within my head
My heart fights back in a push me pull me,
a tug of war where I reach out to my love ones
to share the demons attacking me.
Unfortunately for Lek, my sweat mate,
the demons take over my voice
promising the killing of the evil cops,
those responsible for impeding freedom
by enforcing asinine rules made by politicians
with bulging wallets thanks to industrial friends.

Psychotic neurons bouncing off
my skull repel arguments to slow down.
Even slow deep breaths, messengers of serenity
get firebombed with emotional particles
bursting out of their confines.
Soon my brain controls my body,
adrenaline rushes throughout,
causing me to tense up, to shout
"Kill, kill, kill" at no one in particular.
A word on the wall, anger rings of truth
and justifies the look of destruction
I impose on anyone unlucky to cross my path.

I just wait for the police to arrive
So they can draw their guns, I must match them
Shoot the uninjured one and take out my knife
To surgically remove his skin,
forcing his own flesh and blood
Down his mouth so he chokes in red disgust.
A piece of meat who needs to be taught a lesson.
I am a teacher, the judge, the executioner.
He must die because he is a policeman,
yet, I won't do it from my padded cell.

BOOTS TO HEELS

Marching with my crisp beret
after 20 months of training.
Carried all my gear to stand
my ground after the towers of freedom fell.

Boots to honor the flag raised above
brave brothers and sisters in dust covered
browns and greens. I saved the bodies
of fellow soldiers dusty, dry, and cold.

Some of my brothers with boots lead me to injury,
not from those we wanted to destroy,
rather by those participating in the mission
to stand firm against the enemy within.

A battle between the sexes, with no Foxhole
to evade emotionally lethal advances
Now I am trying to find my way home.
Fighting sadness, depressed with blood

splattered flashbacks, hallucinating bone
crunching music. Duty and circumstance
on this dark journey to light. Master of my destiny.
Time to glow and shine, flourish

as a soldier who serves in glory the star
and splendor stripes filled with belief
in the mission and dedication to my brothers
and sisters in boots only to feel abandoned.

Back in the world of heels, I seek to remove my boots.
Turning to art and song, my outlet that won't
blame me for being there to do my duty
at the wrong time when friendly fire held me down.

SPOOKED

Those cicadas were amplified
as I approached the compound,
a fort like house with ten-foot walls
topped with electrified barbed wire.

The tropical night got louder with chirps
The sweat stinging my eyes.
Even louder... Wait...
It is quiet, under the moonless sky

dark and still attacked by the blood
throbbing in my head.
No aspirin could ease me
as I slide past the guard.

The spooks continue to move
through the night silent
completing their dark task
as if G-d had sent them to meet the first born.

An explosion silences all
Except the ringing in my head
As I crawl out with singed clothes
and blistering skin in this moonlit night

Shadows from the flames scream.
Screams and more screams startle me
The cloudy skies glow a double edge
With a blade dulled on fear and loss,

Where, where am I?
My partner's blood dries on my hands,
Spilled not by me, sliced by another.
Or so it seems, I think, or do I?

Perhaps she moved forward,
involving someone else. She left
to clean up her blistering pains
Around her lips, which I had given her

She stormed out with fiery words
directed at me. My intel failed
I had not plan to be abandoned.
Now crawling towards evacuation and... out

ICEBERG

On the cliffs of an icy landscape,
the edges of my heart crumble
with each passing day. Cold chunks fall
into a stormy Antarctic Sea. My barren
spirit shivers from the chilling winds
as they penetrate deep into my bones.

I tense up, shivering in an attempt
to generate warmth within my spirit.
The birds have flown north, the sea life
have dived deep, away from the scarred
debris falling into the gray ocean
rolling with capsizing swells.

Your rejection has hardened the pure
white droplets into a long, slippery dream.
Yet pieces break away with each moment,
leaving jagged rocks exposed.
I pray for this iceberg of passion to melt
before the elements wear deep crevices in my face.

ABSENT MINDED

They say, or so I surmise,
that the absent-minded fool
forgets his key on purpose,
yet being easily distracted
by flirtatious thoughts
and wanton looks
from the woman with
the red V-neck blouse
keeps his fantasies flowing
with one more drink
mixed with interest.

Now I have lost my keys and can't
let myself into my house
where I've collected keepsakes,
heart shaped bottles,
empty of cognac and other pleasures,
keepsakes of you for these past years.

I sneak to the backyard,
where we once exchanged vows.
Now, the ground is fertilized with guilt.
I barely remember why I forgot to water
the seeds of our relationship.
All I want is to synchronize
the past with the present and move
back inside the home we built.

TRADITIONAL BAR BLUES

The bluesy vocals of old love
echo themes of broken trust
throughout this empty dark dive
where beer is cheap and songs
confuse reality with facts.
Dark glasses and a hat
cover my escape into the music.
I close my eyes and lean back to the past;
discordant love pulls me under
the table during the electric guitar solo.
Beer spills sorrow on the stained wood table
vibrating rhythms as our bed
once danced to our favorite tune
sung in another key.
The music's finished; the bar's shut down.
Lonely people walk home fast, and lovers stroll,
or is it reversed in this dim part of town?

SHADOW OF A DARK HOUSE

Shadow of a dark house dances
in the afternoon sun.
It's cardboard walls sway
with the music of the wind
and the snare pounds out wet
rhythms from the gray sky.
A man wearing the same sport's coat
he found five years ago
conducts his affairs like a refugee
from pestering police and thieves.
Inside he pulls a ripped blanket
over his shoulder and waits for
the afternoon shadows to stretch
themselves alongside him.
He takes out his Aladdin's bottle
and lets the magic spirit
warm the celebration. A toast, "To life!"
That is all.

DRIVING

Driving down the coast,
lost on the planet,
a voyage away from friends,
forced from family by their denial
that I have taken the wrong path.
I search for the road
that connects harmony with
the depressed pieces of myself.

Five pennies on the car seat
one for love,
one for a job,
one for the self,
one for friends,
one to live,
enough to make a nickel,
yet not enough even for a telephone call.
All I can do is save this cash
until I see a place to stop the car
and enjoy spending my money.

Decisions are difficult on an
empty stomach.
Disjointed thoughts
connected by a thread,
woven with a shaky soul,
needles my imagination
with a stake driven into my heart.
I think I'll buy a steak with the
extra money in the coffee cup holder.

SUNSET BOULEVARD

An invalid lives in the glamour part of town
where young prostitutes
switch childhood for disease.
Dusk draws him into the pedestrian lane;
rolling west, as if trying to catch
the falling sun. He stares
at the girls who glance at him.
Luxury cars stop in front of the girls;
then, steering the wheels of pleasure,
ephemeral couples drive away.

The sun sets as the earth turns
towards darkness, and the invalid
edges closer to another girl
everyday, trying to be part of her life,
standing his chair up on its rear wheels
as once he did as a motorcyclist.
He jokes with some of the girls,
asking them if they would valet park
his stalled vehicle before tow trucks
pull him into the night. Shadow of a dark house.

EMPTY VESSEL

Empty, hollow on the inside,
worn patches of plaque plug gaps
where love once freely flowed, carrying
sustaining oxygen on vibrant blood cells.

The void stretches throughout
my body, now a shell of the past.
Why did I believe that I would always be there.
Decayed trails of time remain to be disposed.

LEADHEAD

I repeat the scene in my head,
not ever getting out of bed.
I lie naked as when I checked in,
ready to face my next of kin.

Before the squeeze, the lead chunk waits
in cold steel, messenger of fate.
I call the doctor to kill the pain
with one steady shot to the brain.

RECOVERY

CHOICES

The wind cannot overturn a mountain.
nor temptation touch the man
with the knowledge that his choices
control his desire or that he too will pass.

Remove desire and harvest the strength
of nature among tempestuous roots
which plunge deep into pure soil
that allow the heart to love
and the mind to speak even though
desire muddies awareness of right and wrong.

Salvation resides in awareness of the heart's
choices, where control stands firm
and flourishes year-round. The harvest
approaches for those who focus
on uprooting the weeds of desire
and tending to budding plants.

PASSION FRUIT

This passion filled plant yields fruits
sweet and sour, ripe and unripe
underneath wrapping vines,
blocking out the sun but not the heat.

Fallen, shriveled, purple shells
have created craters in the ground.
with words built from displaced soil
wrapped around the banks.
I once embedded the same words
on your Valentine's day card.

The words printed express previously
unmentioned feelings and desires.
"All the world I want
shines in your eyes,
lives in your smile,
and is held in your hands.
All the world I want
Is your love."

On this harvest day,
I promise to take care
of your well being, forever.
I have given you my heart
Please take care of it.

Like fading emotions, the words,
meanings in language,
weather with time, blurred ink
that looks like decaying fruit.
Yet somehow, they never leave
because new fruit sprouts
from seeds, the same passion
filled vines year after year.

AWAY AT SEA

PART I

I roll across my bunk with each new wave
and back again and again, another roll,
another roll. I curl up with hot dreams
amidst an iceberg laden Arctic Sea.

The time for love yields to patriotic duty.
We patrol, playing hide and seek
with the fiery red devil
on the opposite side of the world.

The armored ship covers my emotions
from the frothing swells and empty troughs
as I hide under cover with memories
of your warm body laying next to me.

A burst of passion flashes across the sky
to ignite my soul's metal.
The smell of burnt gun powder fills my lungs
with smoldering remains of yesterday's love.

PART II

I've been relieved after eighteen hours
of duty and watches. I wander down
the passage way; the same passage way
I walk each day from my rack
to my job and back to my spongy rack.

Did I pass anyone in the narrow corridor?
I crawl onto the cramp and dark bunk.
I dream of you waiting for me.
Crash! The guardrail bruises me.
I babble curses for being confined to long
distance fantasies as I drift away...

Four hours later I shiver in the shower
while cursing myself for volunteering for sea duty.
What were you doing last night my love?
Who did you party with? Were you faithful?
Are you still waiting for me?
Do you miss me? I long for you.
Are you faithful to me?

The blue water engulfs my swelling thoughts
of you sleeping with another man.
I sink below the surface of this irrational storm
deeper and deeper into frantic jealousy.
I splash and grab for any solid object
among a vast mass of spiraling water.

PART III

The chaplain throws a spiritual lifesaver,
and I instinctively grab hold of his words.
He reminds me that she wonders
what I'm doing,
if I miss her,
if I'm okay,
and when she will get to see me again.

He offers me a little faith to warm my spirit
and cup of tea to soothe my soul.

The ship returns home to awaken the dawn,
a new morning to greet old faces.
We anchor, secure from sea detail,
and I'm off the ship into her arms.
Let's go have a drink
to celebrate our reunion.
We squeeze one another, kiss one another,
and look long into each other's eyes.

In bed we rest, and I remember
My hot bunk, thinking about you,
how wonderful I thought you were.
And now I know how right I am.

WINE BOTTLE

EMPTIED

The uncorked bottle of red wine freely flows
among the guests. I empty my glass and realize
my desire to fill it with your vintage year,
only to discover that you have poured all the wine

from the bottle. My heart craves another sip
of your sweet pleasures. I remember toasting
our future and celebrating our present
with an unlimited supply from our cellar.

All you can offer me now is an old cork
and words that our love needs more aging
before you will even consider allowing me
to stick my corkscrew into our bottle of passion.

Our love may mature, but you claim time
to let the sediment settle after I shook you up
and hurt you by not filtering the truth,
leaving a lie to solidify in the bottle.

FILLED

I have repaired my cellar for proper aging,
and declare our love ageless. Lost
and emptiness spill from my soul as you decide
whether or not to replenish our passion,

I have reserved a space in my heart for your future
vintages, a sweet blend from the ripe fruit
of our seeds. I patiently wait to see
how the wine develops within our bottle.

DRUNK

The fermented fruit has matured
When I slip the screw in and pull
out the cork. Filling both our glasses
and toast our fine vintage, a ripe bouquet

that time has softened the harsh tannins,
complex flavors, to a smooth blend.
I swagger through the cellar, seeking to
embrace your sweetness one more time.

WALKING ON CLOUDS

Tornadoes of emotion let the pain explode
in a raging wind swirling around my head.
The rhythm pounds chunks of icy rain
on those I love. These tempestuous emotions block
my confidence as I climb elusive rocks up
to the clouds. The steep path warrants a team effort.

I wake up from a daze and find myself several
years older, filled with the vigor I remember
from youth. Climbing to the sky, I continue
my lifelong quest to walk on the clouds.
Loving you has catalyzed my true nature
to emerge from a dormant state on this mountain of life.

Now I climb alone, and I notice room on this path
for you by my side. Come with me as tender harmony
fills the jagged edges laying ahead for us to climb
over before we reach the walkway among the clouds.
My love for you steadies our path upwards,
my dear, the journey is our shared pleasure.

TURTLE

The turtle swims to the banks of the stream,
bringing good luck to the human visitor.
Do you remember the one I gave you
while you sat in your robe,
lazing on your parents's sofa
during the Loi Kratong festival?

To show my love for you, I bought
a cast metal turtle while we vacationed
in Monterey. The stuffed white turtle
brought peace and love on Valentine's day,
The green stuff turtle was a request
for forgiveness when I raised my voice
and yelled at you for not doing what I wanted.
I slipped three fingers into that soft puppet,
touching your neck and ear with a gentle
offering to restore our friendship.

Dozens of ornamental turtles,
gifts from me to keep our luck alive
placed on a shelf, their home.

SAILING THE SEA OF DREAMS

I
The water, warm with innocence,
reflects the sun's soothing rays,
lighting my ship's path
bright as the north star.
I imagine a solo course, west,
to a new world filled with foreign names
I once read in adventure stories.
I fill the cargo hull with fresh water and food,
haul in the gangplank,
coil the ropes,
and gently glide away.
I've dreamed of this sailing birth
long ago, in a banker's life
of living and managing someone else's dreams.
I leave the soft hum in the serene harbor
to meet a windy new world past the breakwater.
I cry out with a brave scream
when the brisk air slaps me
out of my sheltered warmth.

I race around the buoys
and play chess with the weekend sailors
on board their yachts; we mix
our energies with bottled effervescence
and a toast to the great mother earth.

A tuna boat returns to land
and serves free food by the cupful
to all the sport fishing gulls
following it home.
My heart freezes
for a moment
as I see the present fade
with the dying shore,
and I am alone.

The tuna boat's fresh wake reminds me
of finished discussions
with family, friends, and a lover,
lost forever.

An empty horizon
separates the sky
from the doldrums flat blue sea.
There!
Dry rocks,
an Island
void
of life,
sunken in cloudy water,
a wasteland waiting for a wind
of thoughts, fertile seeds.

The blue fresh water of my eyes
cools my temperature

and cleanses my senses,

letting me see and smell and feel

the gull's destiny,

his endless quest for food.

A dolphin school flashes bright

streaks across the sea surface

and guides my spirit through the stale water

yo the sea's collective wisdom.

The dolphins lead me to the charcoal remains

of a floating burnt out ship,

rotting and corroding in timeless death.

I read the Ophelia's captain's log.

The crew had cooked a gull

then set the ship ablaze in the salty purgatory.

Her drenched hull waits to sink

and then to be reborn as a reef.

II

I spot a maiden in her own sailing vessel.

I steer closer and holler hello.

She welcomes me and explains her flight

from a slow and cumbersome battleship

piloted by her ex-lover.

She and I race with pleasure,

towing each other along,

In and out through coral atolls

where we dive in playful dreams

colored with rare fish.

On board her ship, I lose my helm

to the pursuing battleship
of her jealous ex-boyfriend
whom I had ignored.
He declares war with mind games.
Fiery energy shells explode
in between her and I,
and the sea rages
up in disturbing response;
each wave's forceful crash
lingers
until the next wave surges
with devilish vibrations
lurking behind his evil eye.
Stunned, wet, without hope
nor desire, I float on the sea's now icy surface.

My sister's ship luckily sails by
and rescues me from the stormy seas.
I change into dry clothes and fall asleep.
I plunge deep into dream time,
afloat on the subdued waves
of a tranquil sea
and open my soul's serene door
then sink deeper into my subconscious,
hunting for ancient clues
to unify my former lives.

I remember a previous storm:
A hazy time in a land locked life,
a dim year stuck in dusk.

The typhoon struck during an eclipsing moon;
the violence leaked inside my shelter's heart.
Constant drainage dragged on,
pumping and pouring the muddy sea
out from the basement.
The night lengthened, camouflaged
against a black ocean. That storm
endured a year before I powered through
and beat down the dark night
by bridging innocence and experience.
I patched the leaks and fixed the windmill
to harness the fleeting wind.

My sister leads me back to my ship.
I grab the wheel, again steering
toward the twinkling light
to fuel the powerful light of my heart
which overwhelms the angry darkness.

III
The sun's light walks on the water
and shines mature hope into my eyes.
A gentle breeze wakes me from an ocean of daydreams
where I traversed in my mind.
and looked for the victor
of the dual between fantasy and reality.
I yield my quest to the wind
which carries holy illusions
on earth up to the sky.

93

I scan the horizon
and see her familiar ship
alone.
I send my love a question:
"Are you still travelling my direction?
Can we travel together until we find our port-of-call?"
No? Yet she stays within sight, parallel
with my course,
frequently pretending
to fix position to the land, sea, and sky
while she plots her fiery
charted course with my emotions.
Her ship's mast reflects
strength off the flowing ocean surface,
mirroring
the sun's life-giving energy.
The current pulls her ship closer;
we lock hands and toss our emotional baggage
overboard into the salty graveyard
to be reborn as eternal love.

CLEARING THE SMOKE

Waking from erratic sleep,
I turn off the radio left on last night.
What did the voice from the box
Tell me to do?
"Smoke a cigarette to the last puff?"
I do.

Sluggish,
I move about my world by habit;
I run and sweat and shower.
Another cigarette's smoke filters through me
before circulating into the sky.
I brew inexpensive tea and heat up
two slices of pizza from last night.
My imagination hears her voice
saying, "I need a change."
Anticipating her letter, I smoke a cigarette.

She promised to write six months ago.
The letter arrived with the bills.
She wants to clear the haze
of past affairs before it seeps into her new life.
As I reread the letter, explicating her style,
I smile, I sigh, I begin
my next task: to quit smoking.

CAMPING FOR TWO

We giggle under a star filled night, our
arms holding our souls in close unison.
My lips taste yours as comet trails cross
the moonlit sky. We hold hands and close our eyes.

The misty mountain air allows the rising
light to seep into our tent and greet us
with the warmth of a new day. I look down
at your relaxed face, half asleep, yet smiling

as I stroke your cheeks and tell you how much
knowing you invigorates my life with
desires I long thought were the dreams of youth.
I want to wake inside you every day.

From this forested meadow where birds chirp
for a mate and deer forage for food,
The tall and slender grass bends back and forth
an ebb and flow that demands harmony.

As I slide my fingers through your fine hair,
my hand searches ways to give you pleasure.
The clean air purifies my heart as I
propose that we watch the sun climb above.

Rich floral scents and wealthy green pines fill
our senses as we forget last winter
when you nearly starved from the lies I fed
you. Yet now, the truth smiles down on us,

echoing the wake up call of the morning breeze.
My words flow through the leaves confirming
a redeemed heart no longer blind to love.
Even the flowing stream gurgles stronger

when I gaze deep into your sparkling eyes
and tell you, "I celebrate each morning
and thank God for allowing us to find
each other in this wilderness of life.

SUKOTHAI

I seek my new best friend, this new year day,
who has eluded me for the span of my life.
The loss and regrets of life still haunt me
Filling my heart, causing the palpitations to throb
more strongly, awakening the progress of time.
A letter to my ex-wife, to let her know how much

I miss her and refuse to let her memories evaporate
In the desert heat. Clinging to what could have been,
A life filled sounds of children growing into adults
to carry forth our legacy of love and family
with a best friend, a companion, a true mate.
To share the best and worst life has.

Now pretending to move forward in an ancient city.
Stopping to remember a fleeting memory
Locked in time, cherished in my charade.
The purpose I sought has eluded me
With tempered delusions of grandeur.
No happiness to satisfy longings, a quiet Buddha statue.

Come my friend and escort me to relief
take away the pain, a fleeting memory
of time, crumbling ruins of an ancient society
the former capital, like Sukohthai, now left in disarray
and shambles decomposing granite, void of life.
If you take me now, I will not argue or fight.

NO PAIN, NO GAIN

Tight muscles contract, pulling pain
Close and pushing it away.
Setting the weight down
Release of building tension,

They say no pain, no gain;
Although I thought that the expression
Referred to exercise, creating stress
Where the body repairs itself.

Disjointed thoughts connected by
a thread, woven with a shaky soul,
needles my imagination
with a stake driven into my heart.

The weights, think of the weights
Pushed above my face, Clang,
I drop the weights to the bar
my sweat has toughened my heart.

KIM'S SPEECH

With eager eyes, the young nurses,
tomorrow's healthcare workers,
fix their gaze to the podium
as Kim steps up to replace
the monotone administrator
who stumbled through X-rays and charts.

You assure the graduating students
that calm words will sooth
the patients grasping for strength
when faceless death announces
its claim on the terminal person
as he moves on a one-way gurney.

Kim pauses in blind reflection,
oblivious to those eager spirits
in front of her. Gentle red strands
of hair cover her overworked eyes,
stifling the life of her speech
and preventing it from
pumping the fuel of knowledge,

until
she unsheathes her concern for others,
the love of humanity,
the drug of choice, to teach,
to carry on with the commencement
address explaining how to battle

anger,
guilt,
anxiety,
and sorrow
when pain and confusion
overwhelm family and nurses.

A touch of her gentle green eyes,
fertile with wisdom gained from past crises,
replace the cavity of traumatic stress.
Absent words explaining how
to let their hearts heal dying souls
with a warm and vibrant ear.

"All these words," you explain, "took
a lifetime of experience to prepare.
Now go forth and heal from your heart
as there is no pill to sooth the soul."

ABOVE THE CLOUDS

A trap door from the clouds opens
and I ride down a pearly escalator
lubricated with life's fluid.
I come from dreams of heavenly skies
onto a mountain firm with love.

You lay there on a rocky bed
where all the other stormy souls
succumb to flesh's frozen passion.
I lift your glowing spirit up
over the silver lined threshold
and escort you above the clouds.

NEW DAY

Strong gazes at the craters on the moon
I walk through the night air, still and quiet,
wondering which reality is true and which is not.

The stars I speak about my piercing past
as I look for the moon light to guide my steps
through hours of wandering on the edge of town.

The dawn star asks me why I hold pain
when life awakens song and fresh dew
mixed with tears. My eyes open to another day.

PICA MAN

I am

the soul

who thrives

I smell I

S M I L E

Eat

talk then sing loud songs

of comedy and soft tunes of sadness

inspired by my

limited body

until I change

by growing fatter

and richer in wisdom

then I and
sag
shr-   ivel

as   a leg

hid-   ing a

nest   of

vari-   cose

veins   above

worn   shoes

GOD'S SPECTRUM

Truth's ever changing vanishing point redeems
human beings sealed in skin
when time chafes away distant dreams
and reveals there is no original sin.

DREAMS AND OTHER ELEMENTS OF DUSK

As the dusk swallows the life of day,
a crumbling sand castle challenges
the incoming waves of time. Another breaker
crashes on the gritty shore's ephemeral life,
weathering away at pure monument,
a day's work for the boy who went home
to fall asleep.

Dreams and other elements of dusk
reflect the sadness I once felt
before I became eternally hardened
for my descendants to gaze at,
with traces of my life and age.

Did I leave them enough to know
that mankind's face changes, but black
hearts and dusty dreams linger,
wanting to dominate those who still remain alive.

What hope should be cherished,
or can be innocently imagined
by the wondering thoughts of children
or the intellectual critic in this museum?

A small plaque, bronze words that praise
the sculptor for capturing my wandering soul,
reflects the dimming light as colors deepen.
It's time to lock the door and enter the night.

POSTERITY

COLLECTED EPIGRAMS

Time provides a different frame
of reference for the same event.

Words are my children
as I give birth to a poem,
pure in heart, as
innocence sheds with age.

Someway, somehow, I'll find a way
To turn my dream world into reality.
In the meanwhile, I'll stick to gold and lead.

If you do not eat bugs,
what's that lobster doing in the pot?

If you are afraid of spiders,
why are you dipping your
cracker into that crab dip?

Here lies truth covered up by facts.

Pollution:
Flesh rips from shattering bones;
Both disperse in the air.
What is left falls to world peace.

They call me the rotten apple.
By the way, here is an empty Snapple
bottle that will still be waiting to decompose
long after I have finished.

Create excitement by adding positive energy.
Stop living, and excitement dies.

The pen is mightier then the sword.
What is mite, but a small insect?

Disjointed thoughts
connected by a thread,
woven with a shaky soul,
needles my imagination
covering the body
trimmed by emotional scissors.

About the Author

Dr. Steven H Kaplan, NMD Graduated from Sonoran Univesity Health Sciens with Naturopathic Medical Degree, He heared His master of Arts in Radio-TV-film from California State University Northridge, where he was Graduate student of the year. He earned his Bachelor's degree at UCLA with a major in English Literature.

He currently practices Naturopathic medicine In Phoenix. Prior to that he he worked in IT and video as a Project manager, producer, director, writer. He has been adjunct faculty at several universities, and colleges. He worked in Advertising and various media productions, including helping to create the first DVD-ROM released commercially in US. He taught US sailors onboard USN naval vessels, owned a travel business sending people to Malaysian Borneo, and volunteered in the refugee camps in Thailand, helping various SE Asian refugees.

Dr. Kaplan was awarded a Certificate of Recognition from the California State Legislature for his efforts and contributions to the PAL organization in Los Angeles. He has been the winner of a critical writing award at the graduate level, as well as the heritage of excellence award at California State University, Northridge. He also has 50 hours of service to the Veterans Administration in Sepulveda, California. Her founded and runs a non-profit organization called Asian Festival. He is originally from Los Angeles, and now lives in Phoenix.

Acknowledgments

I express deep gratitude to everyone I met who helped me to learn various Life lessons. My parents, who encouraged me to be creative, the women I have loved, my family who have always tolerated me, my friends who helped keep me focused during emotional ups and downs.

Made in the USA
Middletown, DE
04 September 2024